# The
# ENCHANTING FAIRIES
# COLORING BOOK

SIRIUS

**SIRIUS**

This edition published in 2024 by Sirius Publishing, a division of
Arcturus Publishing Limited,
26/27 Bickels Yard, 151–153 Bermondsey Street,
London SE1 3HA

ISBN: 978-1-3988-4317-2
CH012420NT
Supplier 29, Date 0224, PI 00006694

Printed in China

Created for children 10+

# Introduction

Fairies are mythical creatures found in the folklore of many nations and storytelling traditions. Most have wings and are considered to have magic powers. Some are associated with particular fruits or berries or types of flowers, and their behavior or how they appear will reflect this. Shakespeare included fairies—or spirits similar to them—in some of his most famous plays: the playful Puck in *A Midsummer Night's Dream* and the trapped Ariel in *The Tempest*.

The fairies in this romantic collection of images are inspired by the delicate winged creatures beloved of illustrators such as Arthur Rackham, Edmund Dulac, and Margaret Tarrant, as well as the beautiful artworks created by Pre-Raphaelite painters such as Dante Gabriel Rossetti and Edward Burne-Jones.

You can choose to color them any way you wish, whether your preference is for pastels or bolder tones. Just choose your favorite place to relax, make a selection of colored pencils or pens and begin to create your own fairytale image.

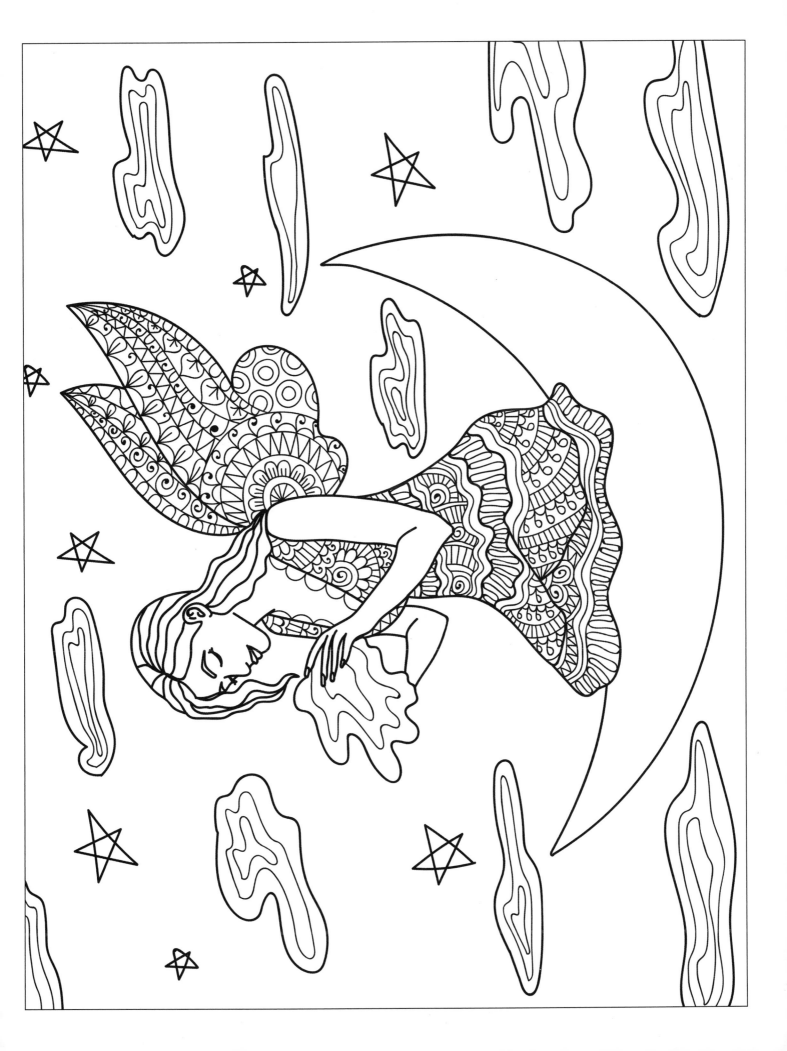